Self-Care Journal

Self-Care Journal

Daily reflections
for mind, body,
and soul

EMMA VAN HINSBERGH

ARCTURUS

All images courtesy of Shutterstock.

ARCTURUS
This edition published in 2024 by Arcturus Publishing Limited
26/27 Bickels Yard, 151–153 Bermondsey Street,
London SE1 3HA

ISBN: 978-1-3988-3936-6
AD011857NT

Printed in China

 # INTRODUCTION

You don't have to check into a five-star spa to treat yourself; you should be actively nurturing your mind, body, and soul from the minute you wake up until the moment you go to sleep at night.

The gentle holistic art of self-care is all about being proactive when it comes to maintaining harmony and balance in your life; about taking actions to improve your physical, mental, and emotional wellbeing. Self-care is about recognizing the importance of your own needs and making a dedicated effort toward achieving them in order to nurture a positive relationship with yourself. By doing this, you can improve every aspect of your life, from reducing stress and boosting self-esteem to enhancing productivity and improving your interactions with people.

Research shows that self-care contributes to increased resilience, better overall health and wellbeing, and a better ability to manage life's challenges, so making it top of to do your list should be a daily priority.

On a physical level this means anything from eating nourishing wholefoods to exercising regularly. Or maybe taking an occasional break from social media or technology and making sure you get quality sleep. On an emotional level it can mean treating yourself with compassion, incorporating loving kindness meditations such as "May I be happy, may I be healthy, may I be safe, may I be at ease," into your daily routine. On a social level it could mean connecting friends and family or pursuing your hobbies, while on a spiritual level it could mean engaging in self-reflection and cultivating a habit of gratitude, acknowledging the blessings in your life, or maybe connecting with nature by going for a walk in the park or a swim in the sea.

Self-care can also take the form of relaxing rituals such as treating yourself to a pampering spa day occasionally, reading a book, listening to music, or soaking in a warm bath laced with aromatherapy oils. Even having regular medical check-ups and visiting your dental hygienist is looking after yourself in a proactive and positive manner and will reap rewards on many levels.

So, nurture a flourishing relationship with yourself every day and remind yourself to work on your wellbeing by writing down on paper all the steps you have taken to build on this every day.

Use this beautiful journal to write down every little act of kindness and remember that self-care is not a luxury but a fundamental aspect toward leading a healthier and happier life. Remember to be gentle with yourself as you turn the page to start your self-care journey now...

Good Morning

Set your intentions to reinforce a health and positive mindset the moment you wake up and repeat this morning meditation mantra: "I start this day with love for myself, I am mindful of my wellbeing, and I will make choices for a healthy and balanced life."

DAILY CHECK-IN

Mind
I will nurture and build my emotional health and resilience by...

....

....

Body
I will nourish, celebrate, and empower my body by...

....

....

Soul
I will create moments of tranquility, peace, and harmony by...

....

....

I will find harmony and balance in nature by...

....

....

....

I set a positive intention to...

....

....

....

Sweet Dreams

Before you go to sleep at night, light a scented candle,
put on some calming music, and take some time out for reflection...

What I loved and appreciated about myself today was...

....

....

The negative thoughts that I release are...

....

....

REFLECTIONS

Three moments that brought
joy, laughter or a sense of
fulfilment were...

1 ....

   ....

2 ....

   ....

3 ....

   ....

My good night meditation mantra...
"I will focus on my breath,
allowing it to be a source of calm
and balance. I inhale positive
energy and exhale any tension or
negativity as I drift off to sleep."

Good Morning

Date ___ / ___ / ___

Set your intentions to reinforce a health and positive mindset the moment you wake up and repeat this morning meditation mantra: "I start this day with love for myself, I am mindful of my wellbeing, and I will make choices for a healthy and balanced life."

DAILY CHECK-IN

Mind
I will nurture and build my emotional health and resilience by...

....

....

Body
I will nourish, celebrate, and empower my body by...

....

....

Soul
I will create moments of tranquility, peace, and harmony by...

....

....

I will find harmony and balance in nature by...

....

....

....

I set a positive intention to...

....

....

....

Sweet Dreams

Before you go to sleep at night, light a scented candle,
put on some calming music, and take some time out for reflection...

What I loved and appreciated about myself today was...

The negative thoughts that I release are...

REFLECTIONS

Three moments that brought
joy, laughter or a sense of
fulfilment were...

1 ....

2 ....

3 ....

My good night meditation mantra...
"I will focus on my breath,
allowing it to be a source of calm
and balance. I inhale positive
energy and exhale any tension or
negativity as I drift off to sleep."

Good Morning

Date ___ / ___ / ___

Set your intentions to reinforce a health and positive mindset the moment you wake up and repeat this morning meditation mantra: "I start this day with love for myself, I am mindful of my wellbeing, and I will make choices for a healthy and balanced life."

DAILY CHECK-IN

Mind
I will nurture and build my emotional health and resilience by...

....

....

Body
I will nourish, celebrate, and empower my body by...

....

....

Soul
I will create moments of tranquility, peace, and harmony by...

....

....

I will find harmony and balance in nature by...

....

....

....

I set a positive intention to...

....

....

....

Sweet Dreams

Before you go to sleep at night, light a scented candle,
put on some calming music, and take some time out for reflection...

What I loved and appreciated about myself today was...

....

....

The negative thoughts that I release are...

....

....

REFLECTIONS

Three moments that brought
joy, laughter or a sense of
fulfilment were...

1 ....

....

2 ....

....

3 ....

....

My good night meditation mantra...
"I will focus on my breath,
allowing it to be a source of calm
and balance. I inhale positive
energy and exhale any tension or
negativity as I drift off to sleep."

Good Morning

Set your intentions to reinforce a health and positive mindset the moment you wake up and repeat this morning meditation mantra: "I start this day with love for myself, I am mindful of my wellbeing, and I will make choices for a healthy and balanced life."

DAILY CHECK-IN

Mind
I will nurture and build my emotional health and resilience by...

....

....

Body
I will nourish, celebrate, and empower my body by...

....

....

Soul
I will create moments of tranquility, peace, and harmony by...

....

....

I will find harmony and balance in nature by...

....

....

I set a positive intention to...

....

....

Sweet Dreams

Before you go to sleep at night, light a scented candle,
put on some calming music, and take some time out for reflection...

What I loved and appreciated about myself today was...

....

....

The negative thoughts that I release are...

....

....

REFLECTIONS

Three moments that brought
joy, laughter or a sense of
fulfilment were...

1 ....

....

2 ....

....

3 ....

....

My good night meditation mantra...
"I will focus on my breath,
allowing it to be a source of calm
and balance. I inhale positive
energy and exhale any tension or
negativity as I drift off to sleep."

Good Morning

Set your intentions to reinforce a health and positive mindset the moment you wake up and repeat this morning meditation mantra: "I start this day with love for myself, I am mindful of my wellbeing, and I will make choices for a healthy and balanced life."

DAILY CHECK-IN

Mind
I will nurture and build my emotional health and resilience by...

....

....

Body
I will nourish, celebrate, and empower my body by...

....

....

Soul
I will create moments of tranquility, peace, and harmony by...

....

....

I will find harmony and balance in nature by...

....

....

....

I set a positive intention to...

....

....

....

16

Sweet Dreams

Before you go to sleep at night, light a scented candle,
put on some calming music, and take some time out for reflection...

What I loved and appreciated about myself today was...

....

....

The negative thoughts that I release are...

....

....

REFLECTIONS

Three moments that brought
joy, laughter or a sense of
fulfilment were...

1 ....

....

2 ....

....

3 ....

....

My good night meditation mantra...
"I will focus on my breath,
allowing it to be a source of calm
and balance. I inhale positive
energy and exhale any tension or
negativity as I drift off to sleep."

Good Morning

Set your intentions to reinforce a health and positive mindset the moment you wake up and repeat this morning meditation mantra: "I start this day with love for myself, I am mindful of my wellbeing, and I will make choices for a healthy and balanced life."

DAILY CHECK-IN

Mind
I will nurture and build my emotional health and resilience by...

....

....

Body
I will nourish, celebrate, and empower my body by...

....

....

Soul
I will create moments of tranquility, peace, and harmony by...

....

....

I will find harmony and balance in nature by...

....

....

....

I set a positive intention to...

....

....

....

Sweet Dreams

Before you go to sleep at night, light a scented candle,
put on some calming music, and take some time out for reflection...

What I loved and appreciated about myself today was...

....

....

The negative thoughts that I release are...

....

....

REFLECTIONS

Three moments that brought
joy, laughter or a sense of
fulfilment were...

1 ....

....

2 ....

....

3 ....

....

My good night meditation mantra...
"I will focus on my breath,
allowing it to be a source of calm
and balance. I inhale positive
energy and exhale any tension or
negativity as I drift off to sleep."

Good Morning

Set your intentions to reinforce a health and positive mindset the moment you wake up and repeat this morning meditation mantra: "I start this day with love for myself, I am mindful of my wellbeing, and I will make choices for a healthy and balanced life."

DAILY CHECK-IN

Mind
I will nurture and build my emotional health and resilience by...

....

....

Body
I will nourish, celebrate, and empower my body by...

....

....

Soul
I will create moments of tranquility, peace, and harmony by...

....

....

I will find harmony and balance in nature by...

....

....

....

I set a positive intention to...

....

....

....

Sweet Dreams

Before you go to sleep at night, light a scented candle,
put on some calming music, and take some time out for reflection...

What I loved and appreciated about myself today was...

....

....

The negative thoughts that I release are...

....

....

REFLECTIONS

Three moments that brought
joy, laughter or a sense of
fulfilment were...

1 ....

....

2 ....

....

3 ....

....

My good night meditation mantra...
"I will focus on my breath,
allowing it to be a source of calm
and balance. I inhale positive
energy and exhale any tension or
negativity as I drift off to sleep."

Good Morning

Date ___ / ___ / ___

Set your intentions to reinforce a health and positive mindset the moment you wake up and repeat this morning meditation mantra: "I start this day with love for myself, I am mindful of my wellbeing, and I will make choices for a healthy and balanced life."

DAILY CHECK-IN

Mind
I will nurture and build my emotional health and resilience by...

....

....

Body
I will nourish, celebrate, and empower my body by...

....

....

Soul
I will create moments of tranquility, peace, and harmony by...

....

....

I will find harmony and balance in nature by...

....

....

I set a positive intention to...

....

....

Sweet Dreams

Before you go to sleep at night, light a scented candle,
put on some calming music, and take some time out for reflection...

What I loved and appreciated about myself today was...

....

....

The negative thoughts that I release are...

....

....

REFLECTIONS

Three moments that brought
joy, laughter or a sense of
fulfilment were...

1 ....

....

2 ....

....

3 ....

....

My good night meditation mantra...
"I will focus on my breath,
allowing it to be a source of calm
and balance. I inhale positive
energy and exhale any tension or
negativity as I drift off to sleep."

Good Morning

Set your intentions to reinforce a health and positive mindset the moment you wake up and repeat this morning meditation mantra: "I start this day with love for myself, I am mindful of my wellbeing, and I will make choices for a healthy and balanced life."

DAILY CHECK-IN

Mind
I will nurture and build my emotional health and resilience by...

....

....

Body
I will nourish, celebrate, and empower my body by...

....

....

Soul
I will create moments of tranquility, peace, and harmony by...

....

....

I will find harmony and balance in nature by...

....

....

I set a positive intention to...

....

....

Sweet Dreams

Before you go to sleep at night, light a scented candle,
put on some calming music, and take some time out for reflection...

What I loved and appreciated about myself today was...

....

....

The negative thoughts that I release are...

....

....

REFLECTIONS

Three moments that brought
joy, laughter or a sense of
fulfilment were...

1 ....

....

2 ....

....

3 ....

....

My good night meditation mantra...
"I will focus on my breath,
allowing it to be a source of calm
and balance. I inhale positive
energy and exhale any tension or
negativity as I drift off to sleep."

Good Morning

Date ___ / ___ / ___

Set your intentions to reinforce a health and positive mindset the moment you wake up and repeat this morning meditation mantra: "I start this day with love for myself, I am mindful of my wellbeing, and I will make choices for a healthy and balanced life."

DAILY CHECK-IN

Mind
I will nurture and build my emotional health and resilience by...

....

....

Body
I will nourish, celebrate, and empower my body by...

....

....

Soul
I will create moments of tranquility, peace, and harmony by...

....

....

I will find harmony and balance in nature by...

....

....

....

I set a positive intention to...

....

....

....

Sweet Dreams

Before you go to sleep at night, light a scented candle,
put on some calming music, and take some time out for reflection...

What I loved and appreciated about myself today was...

....

....

The negative thoughts that I release are...

....

....

REFLECTIONS

Three moments that brought
joy, laughter or a sense of
fulfilment were...

1 ....

....

2 ....

....

3 ....

....

My good night meditation mantra...
"I will focus on my breath,
allowing it to be a source of calm
and balance. I inhale positive
energy and exhale any tension or
negativity as I drift off to sleep."

Good Morning

Set your intentions to reinforce a health and positive mindset the moment you wake up and repeat this morning meditation mantra: "I start this day with love for myself, I am mindful of my wellbeing, and I will make choices for a healthy and balanced life."

DAILY CHECK-IN

Mind
I will nurture and build my emotional health and resilience by...

....

....

Body
I will nourish, celebrate, and empower my body by...

....

....

Soul
I will create moments of tranquility, peace, and harmony by...

....

....

I will find harmony and balance in nature by...

....

....

I set a positive intention to...

....

....

Sweet Dreams

Before you go to sleep at night, light a scented candle,
put on some calming music, and take some time out for reflection...

What I loved and appreciated about myself today was...

....

....

The negative thoughts that I release are...

....

....

REFLECTIONS

Three moments that brought
joy, laughter or a sense of
fulfilment were...

1 ....

....

2 ....

....

3 ....

....

My good night meditation mantra...
"I will focus on my breath,
allowing it to be a source of calm
and balance. I inhale positive
energy and exhale any tension or
negativity as I drift off to sleep."

Good Morning

Date ___ / ___ / ___

Set your intentions to reinforce a health and positive mindset the moment you wake up and repeat this morning meditation mantra: "I start this day with love for myself, I am mindful of my wellbeing, and I will make choices for a healthy and balanced life."

DAILY CHECK-IN

Mind
I will nurture and build my emotional health and resilience by...

....

....

Body
I will nourish, celebrate, and empower my body by...

....

....

Soul
I will create moments of tranquility, peace, and harmony by...

....

....

I will find harmony and balance in nature by...

....

....

....

I set a positive intention to...

....

....

....

Sweet Dreams

Before you go to sleep at night, light a scented candle,
put on some calming music, and take some time out for reflection...

What I loved and appreciated about myself today was...

....

....

The negative thoughts that I release are...

....

....

REFLECTIONS

Three moments that brought
joy, laughter or a sense of
fulfilment were...

1 ....

....

2 ....

....

3 ....

....

My good night meditation mantra...
"I will focus on my breath,
allowing it to be a source of calm
and balance. I inhale positive
energy and exhale any tension or
negativity as I drift off to sleep."

Good Morning

Set your intentions to reinforce a health and positive mindset the moment you wake up and repeat this morning meditation mantra: "I start this day with love for myself, I am mindful of my wellbeing, and I will make choices for a healthy and balanced life."

DAILY CHECK-IN

Mind
I will nurture and build my emotional health and resilience by...

....

....

Body
I will nourish, celebrate, and empower my body by...

....

....

Soul
I will create moments of tranquility, peace, and harmony by...

....

....

I will find harmony and balance in nature by...

....

....

I set a positive intention to...

....

....

Sweet Dreams

Before you go to sleep at night, light a scented candle,
put on some calming music, and take some time out for reflection...

What I loved and appreciated about myself today was...

....

....

The negative thoughts that I release are...

....

....

REFLECTIONS

Three moments that brought
joy, laughter or a sense of
fulfilment were...

1 ....

....

2 ....

....

3 ....

....

My good night meditation mantra...
"I will focus on my breath,
allowing it to be a source of calm
and balance. I inhale positive
energy and exhale any tension or
negativity as I drift off to sleep."

Good Morning

Date ___ / ___ / ___

Set your intentions to reinforce a health and positive mindset the moment you wake up and repeat this morning meditation mantra: "I start this day with love for myself, I am mindful of my wellbeing, and I will make choices for a healthy and balanced life."

DAILY CHECK-IN

Mind
I will nurture and build my emotional health and resilience by...

....

....

Body
I will nourish, celebrate, and empower my body by...

....

....

Soul
I will create moments of tranquility, peace, and harmony by...

....

....

....

I set a positive

intention to...

I will find harmony and balance in nature by...

....

....

....

....

....

Sweet Dreams

Before you go to sleep at night, light a scented candle,
put on some calming music, and take some time out for reflection...

What I loved and appreciated about myself today was...

....

....

The negative thoughts that I release are...

....

....

REFLECTIONS

Three moments that brought joy,
laughter or a sense of fulfilment were...

1 ....

....

2 ....

....

3 ....

....

**My good night
meditation mantra...**
"I will focus on my breath,
allowing it to be a source of calm
and balance. I inhale positive
energy and exhale any tension or
negativity as I drift off to sleep."

Good Morning

Date ___ / ___ / ___

Set your intentions to reinforce a health and positive mindset the moment you wake up and repeat this morning meditation mantra: "I start this day with love for myself, I am mindful of my wellbeing, and I will make choices for a healthy and balanced life."

DAILY CHECK-IN

Mind
I will nurture and build my emotional health and resilience by...

....

....

Body
I will nourish, celebrate, and empower my body by...

....

....

Soul
I will create moments of tranquility, peace, and harmony by...

....

....

....

I set a positive
intention to...

I will find harmony and balance in nature by...

....

....

....

Sweet Dreams

Before you go to sleep at night, light a scented candle,
put on some calming music, and take some time out for reflection...

What I loved and appreciated about myself today was...

....

....

The negative thoughts that I release are...

....

....

REFLECTIONS

Three moments that brought joy,
laughter or a sense of fulfilment were...

1 ....

....

2 ....

....

3 ....

....

**My good night
meditation mantra...**
"I will focus on my breath,
allowing it to be a source of calm
and balance. I inhale positive
energy and exhale any tension or
negativity as I drift off to sleep."

Good Morning

Date ___ / ___ / ___

Set your intentions to reinforce a health and positive mindset the moment you wake up and repeat this morning meditation mantra: "I start this day with love for myself, I am mindful of my wellbeing, and I will make choices for a healthy and balanced life."

DAILY CHECK-IN

Mind
I will nurture and build my emotional health and resilience by...

....

....

Body
I will nourish, celebrate, and empower my body by...

....

....

Soul
I will create moments of tranquility, peace, and harmony by...

....

....

....

I set a positive
intention to...

I will find harmony and balance in nature by...

....

....

....

Sweet Dreams

Before you go to sleep at night, light a scented candle,
put on some calming music, and take some time out for reflection...

What I loved and appreciated about myself today was...

....

....

The negative thoughts that I release are...

....

....

REFLECTIONS

Three moments that brought joy,
laughter or a sense of fulfilment were...

1 ....

....

2 ....

....

3 ....

....

**My good night
meditation mantra...**
"I will focus on my breath,
allowing it to be a source of calm
and balance. I inhale positive
energy and exhale any tension or
negativity as I drift off to sleep."

Good Morning

Set your intentions to reinforce a health and positive mindset the moment you wake up and repeat this morning meditation mantra: "I start this day with love for myself, I am mindful of my wellbeing, and I will make choices for a healthy and balanced life."

DAILY CHECK-IN

Mind
I will nurture and build my emotional health and resilience by...

....

....

Body
I will nourish, celebrate, and empower my body by...

....

....

Soul
I will create moments of tranquility, peace, and harmony by...

....

....

....

I set a positive

intention to...

I will find harmony and balance in nature by...

....

....

....

....

....

Sweet Dreams

Before you go to sleep at night, light a scented candle,
put on some calming music, and take some time out for reflection...

What I loved and appreciated about myself today was...

....

....

The negative thoughts that I release are...

....

....

REFLECTIONS

Three moments that brought joy,
laughter or a sense of fulfilment were...

1 ....

....

2 ....

....

3 ....

....

**My good night
meditation mantra...**
"I will focus on my breath,
allowing it to be a source of calm
and balance. I inhale positive
energy and exhale any tension or
negativity as I drift off to sleep."

Good Morning

Date ___ /___ /___

Set your intentions to reinforce a health and positive mindset the moment you wake up and repeat this morning meditation mantra: "I start this day with love for myself, I am mindful of my wellbeing, and I will make choices for a healthy and balanced life."

DAILY CHECK-IN

Mind
I will nurture and build my emotional health and resilience by...

....

....

Body
I will nourish, celebrate, and empower my body by...

....

....

Soul
I will create moments of tranquility, peace, and harmony by...

....

....

....

I will find harmony and balance in nature by...

....

....

....

I set a positive intention to...

....

....

....

Sweet Dreams

Before you go to sleep at night, light a scented candle,
put on some calming music, and take some time out for reflection...

What I loved and appreciated about myself today was...

....

....

The negative thoughts that I release are...

....

....

REFLECTIONS
Three moments that brought joy,
laughter or a sense of fulfilment were...

1 ....

....

2 ....

....

3 ....

....

**My good night
meditation mantra...**
"I will focus on my breath,
allowing it to be a source of calm
and balance. I inhale positive
energy and exhale any tension or
negativity as I drift off to sleep."

Good Morning

Set your intentions to reinforce a health and positive mindset the moment you wake up and repeat this morning meditation mantra: "I start this day with love for myself, I am mindful of my wellbeing, and I will make choices for a healthy and balanced life."

DAILY CHECK-IN

Mind
I will nurture and build my emotional health and resilience by...

....

....

Body
I will nourish, celebrate, and empower my body by...

....

....

Soul
I will create moments of tranquility, peace, and harmony by...

....

....

....

I set a positive
intention to...

I will find harmony and balance in nature by...

....

....

....

....

....

....

Sweet Dreams

Before you go to sleep at night, light a scented candle,
put on some calming music, and take some time out for reflection...

What I loved and appreciated about myself today was...

....

....

The negative thoughts that I release are...

....

....

REFLECTIONS

Three moments that brought joy,
laughter or a sense of fulfilment were...

1 ....

....

2 ....

....

3 ....

....

**My good night
meditation mantra...**
"I will focus on my breath,
allowing it to be a source of calm
and balance. I inhale positive
energy and exhale any tension or
negativity as I drift off to sleep."

Good Morning

Date ___ / ___ / ___

Set your intentions to reinforce a health and positive mindset the moment you wake up and repeat this morning meditation mantra: "I start this day with love for myself, I am mindful of my wellbeing, and I will make choices for a healthy and balanced life."

DAILY CHECK-IN

Mind
I will nurture and build my emotional health and resilience by...

....

....

Body
I will nourish, celebrate, and empower my body by...

....

....

Soul
I will create moments of tranquility, peace, and harmony by...

....

....

....

I will find harmony and balance in nature by...

....

....

....

I set a positive intention to...

....

....

....

46

Sweet Dreams

Before you go to sleep at night, light a scented candle,
put on some calming music, and take some time out for reflection...

What I loved and appreciated about myself today was...

....

....

The negative thoughts that I release are...

....

....

REFLECTIONS

Three moments that brought joy,
laughter or a sense of fulfilment were...

1 ....

....

2 ....

....

3 ....

....

**My good night
meditation mantra...**
"I will focus on my breath,
allowing it to be a source of calm
and balance. I inhale positive
energy and exhale any tension or
negativity as I drift off to sleep."

Good Morning

Set your intentions to reinforce a health and positive mindset the
moment you wake up and repeat this morning meditation mantra:
"I start this day with love for myself, I am mindful of my wellbeing,
and I will make choices for a healthy and balanced life."

DAILY CHECK-IN

Mind
I will nurture and build my emotional health and resilience by...

....

....

Body
I will nourish, celebrate, and empower my body by...

....

....

Soul
I will create moments of tranquility, peace, and harmony by...

....

....

I set a positive

intention to...

I will find harmony and balance in nature by...

....

....

....

....

Sweet Dreams

Before you go to sleep at night, light a scented candle,
put on some calming music, and take some time out for reflection...

What I loved and appreciated about myself today was...

....

....

The negative thoughts that I release are...

....

....

REFLECTIONS

Three moments that brought joy,
laughter or a sense of fulfilment were...

1 ....

....

2 ....

....

3 ....

....

**My good night
meditation mantra...**
"I will focus on my breath,
allowing it to be a source of calm
and balance. I inhale positive
energy and exhale any tension or
negativity as I drift off to sleep."

Good Morning

Date ___ / ___ / ___

Set your intentions to reinforce a health and positive mindset the moment you wake up and repeat this morning meditation mantra: "I start this day with love for myself, I am mindful of my wellbeing, and I will make choices for a healthy and balanced life."

DAILY CHECK-IN

Mind
I will nurture and build my emotional health and resilience by...

....

....

Body
I will nourish, celebrate, and empower my body by...

....

....

Soul
I will create moments of tranquility, peace, and harmony by...

....

....

....

I will find harmony and balance in nature by...

....

....

....

I set a positive intention to...

....

....

....

Sweet Dreams

Before you go to sleep at night, light a scented candle,
put on some calming music, and take some time out for reflection...

What I loved and appreciated about myself today was...

....

....

The negative thoughts that I release are...

....

....

REFLECTIONS

Three moments that brought joy,
laughter or a sense of fulfilment were...

1 ....

....

2 ....

....

3 ....

....

**My good night
meditation mantra...**
"I will focus on my breath,
allowing it to be a source of calm
and balance. I inhale positive
energy and exhale any tension or
negativity as I drift off to sleep."

Good Morning

Set your intentions to reinforce a health and positive mindset the moment you wake up and repeat this morning meditation mantra: "I start this day with love for myself, I am mindful of my wellbeing, and I will make choices for a healthy and balanced life."

DAILY CHECK-IN

Mind
I will nurture and build my emotional health and resilience by...

....

....

Body
I will nourish, celebrate, and empower my body by...

....

....

Soul
I will create moments of tranquility, peace, and harmony by...

....

....

....

I set a positive
intention to...

I will find harmony and balance in nature by...

....

....

....

....

....

....

Sweet Dreams

Before you go to sleep at night, light a scented candle,
put on some calming music, and take some time out for reflection...

What I loved and appreciated about myself today was...

....

....

The negative thoughts that I release are...

....

....

REFLECTIONS
Three moments that brought joy,
laughter or a sense of fulfilment were...

1 ....

....

2 ....

....

3 ....

....

**My good night
meditation mantra...**
"I will focus on my breath,
allowing it to be a source of calm
and balance. I inhale positive
energy and exhale any tension or
negativity as I drift off to sleep."

Good Morning

Date ___ / ___ / ___

Set your intentions to reinforce a health and positive mindset the moment you wake up and repeat this morning meditation mantra: "I start this day with love for myself, I am mindful of my wellbeing, and I will make choices for a healthy and balanced life."

DAILY CHECK-IN

Mind
I will nurture and build my emotional health and resilience by...

....

....

Body
I will nourish, celebrate, and empower my body by...

....

....

Soul
I will create moments of tranquility, peace, and harmony by...

....

....

....

I will find harmony and balance in nature by...

....

....

....

I set a positive intention to...

....

....

....

....

Sweet Dreams

Before you go to sleep at night, light a scented candle,
put on some calming music, and take some time out for reflection...

What I loved and appreciated about myself today was...

....

....

The negative thoughts that I release are...

....

....

REFLECTIONS

Three moments that brought joy,
laughter or a sense of fulfilment were...

1 ....

....

2 ....

....

3 ....

....

**My good night
meditation mantra...**
"I will focus on my breath,
allowing it to be a source of calm
and balance. I inhale positive
energy and exhale any tension or
negativity as I drift off to sleep."

Good Morning

Date ___ / ___ / ___

Set your intentions to reinforce a health and positive mindset the moment you wake up and repeat this morning meditation mantra: "I start this day with love for myself, I am mindful of my wellbeing, and I will make choices for a healthy and balanced life."

DAILY CHECK-IN

Mind
I will nurture and build my emotional health and resilience by...

....

....

Body
I will nourish, celebrate, and empower my body by...

....

....

Soul
I will create moments of tranquility, peace, and harmony by...

....

....

....

I will find harmony and balance in nature by...

....

....

....

I set a positive intention to...

....

....

....

Sweet Dreams

Before you go to sleep at night, light a scented candle,
put on some calming music, and take some time out for reflection...

What I loved and appreciated about myself today was...

....

....

The negative thoughts that I release are...

....

....

REFLECTIONS

Three moments that brought joy,
laughter or a sense of fulfilment were...

1 ....

....

2 ....

....

3 ....

....

**My good night
meditation mantra...**
"I will focus on my breath,
allowing it to be a source of calm
and balance. I inhale positive
energy and exhale any tension or
negativity as I drift off to sleep."

Good Morning

Set your intentions to reinforce a health and positive mindset the moment you wake up and repeat this morning meditation mantra: "I start this day with love for myself, I am mindful of my wellbeing, and I will make choices for a healthy and balanced life."

DAILY CHECK-IN

Mind
I will nurture and build my emotional health and resilience by...

....

....

Body
I will nourish, celebrate, and empower my body by...

....

....

Soul
I will create moments of tranquility, peace, and harmony by...

....

....

....

I will find harmony and balance in nature by...

....

....

....

I set a positive
intention to...

....

....

....

Sweet Dreams

Before you go to sleep at night, light a scented candle,
put on some calming music, and take some time out for reflection...

What I loved and appreciated about myself today was...

....

....

The negative thoughts that I release are...

....

....

REFLECTIONS

Three moments that brought joy,
laughter or a sense of fulfilment were...

1 ....

....

2 ....

....

3 ....

....

**My good night
meditation mantra...**
"I will focus on my breath,
allowing it to be a source of calm
and balance. I inhale positive
energy and exhale any tension or
negativity as I drift off to sleep."

Good Morning

Set your intentions to reinforce a health and positive mindset the
moment you wake up and repeat this morning meditation mantra:
"I start this day with love for myself, I am mindful of my wellbeing,
and I will make choices for a healthy and balanced life."

DAILY CHECK-IN

Mind
I will nurture and build my emotional health and resilience by...

....

Body
I will nourish, celebrate, and empower my body by...

....

Soul
I will create moments of tranquility, peace, and harmony by...

....

I will find harmony and
balance in nature by...

....

....

....

....

....

I set a positive intention to...

....

....

....

....

....

Sweet Dreams

Before you go to sleep at night, light a scented candle,
put on some calming music, and take some time out for reflection...

What I loved and appreciated about myself today was...

....

....

The negative thoughts that I release are...

....

....

REFLECTIONS

Three moments that brought joy, laughter or a sense of fulfilment were...

1 ....

2 ....

3 ....

My good night meditation mantra...
"I will focus on my breath, allowing it
to be a source of calm and balance.
I inhale positive energy and exhale any
tension or negativity as I drift off to sleep."

Good Morning

Set your intentions to reinforce a health and positive mindset the moment you wake up and repeat this morning meditation mantra: "I start this day with love for myself, I am mindful of my wellbeing, and I will make choices for a healthy and balanced life."

DAILY CHECK-IN

Mind
I will nurture and build my emotional health and resilience by...

....

Body
I will nourish, celebrate, and empower my body by...

....

Soul
I will create moments of tranquility, peace, and harmony by...

....

I will find harmony and balance in nature by...

....

....

....

....

I set a positive intention to...

....

....

....

....

Sweet Dreams

Before you go to sleep at night, light a scented candle,
put on some calming music, and take some time out for reflection...

What I loved and appreciated about myself today was...

....

....

The negative thoughts that I release are...

....

....

REFLECTIONS

Three moments that brought joy, laughter or a sense of fulfilment were...

1 ....

2 ....

3 ....

My good night meditation mantra...
"I will focus on my breath, allowing it
to be a source of calm and balance.
I inhale positive energy and exhale any
tension or negativity as I drift off to sleep."

Good Morning

Date ___ /___ /___

Set your intentions to reinforce a health and positive mindset the
moment you wake up and repeat this morning meditation mantra:
"I start this day with love for myself, I am mindful of my wellbeing,
and I will make choices for a healthy and balanced life."

DAILY CHECK-IN

Mind
I will nurture and build my emotional health and resilience by...

....

Body
I will nourish, celebrate, and empower my body by...

....

Soul
I will create moments of tranquility, peace, and harmony by...

....

I will find harmony and
balance in nature by...

....
....
....
....
....
....

I set a positive intention to...

....
....
....
....
....
....

Sweet Dreams

Before you go to sleep at night, light a scented candle,
put on some calming music, and take some time out for reflection...

What I loved and appreciated about myself today was...

....

....

The negative thoughts that I release are...

....

....

REFLECTIONS

Three moments that brought joy, laughter or a sense of fulfilment were...

1 ....

2 ....

3 ....

My good night meditation mantra...
"I will focus on my breath, allowing it
to be a source of calm and balance.
I inhale positive energy and exhale any
tension or negativity as I drift off to sleep."

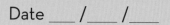

Good Morning

Date ___ / ___ / ___

Set your intentions to reinforce a health and positive mindset the moment you wake up and repeat this morning meditation mantra: "I start this day with love for myself, I am mindful of my wellbeing, and I will make choices for a healthy and balanced life."

DAILY CHECK-IN

Mind
I will nurture and build my emotional health and resilience by...

....

Body
I will nourish, celebrate, and empower my body by...

....

Soul
I will create moments of tranquility, peace, and harmony by...

....

I will find harmony and balance in nature by...

....

....

....

....

I set a positive intention to...

....

....

....

....

....

Sweet Dreams

Before you go to sleep at night, light a scented candle,
put on some calming music, and take some time out for reflection...

>>>>>>>> What I loved and appreciated <<<<<<<<
about myself today was...

....

....

The negative thoughts that I release are...

....

....

REFLECTIONS

Three moments that brought joy, laughter or a sense of fulfilment were...

1 ....

2 ....

3 ....

My good night meditation mantra...
"I will focus on my breath, allowing it
to be a source of calm and balance.
I inhale positive energy and exhale any
tension or negativity as I drift off to sleep."

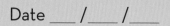

Good Morning

Date ___ / ___ / ___

Set your intentions to reinforce a health and positive mindset the moment you wake up and repeat this morning meditation mantra: "I start this day with love for myself, I am mindful of my wellbeing, and I will make choices for a healthy and balanced life."

DAILY CHECK-IN

Mind
I will nurture and build my emotional health and resilience by...

....

Body
I will nourish, celebrate, and empower my body by...

....

Soul
I will create moments of tranquility, peace, and harmony by...

....

I will find harmony and balance in nature by...

....
....
....
....

I set a positive intention to...

....
....
....
....

Sweet Dreams

Before you go to sleep at night, light a scented candle,
put on some calming music, and take some time out for reflection...

>>>>>>> What I loved and appreciated <<<<<<<
about myself today was...

....

....

The negative thoughts that I release are...

....

....

REFLECTIONS

Three moments that brought joy, laughter or a sense of fulfilment were...

1 ....

2 ....

3 ....

My good night meditation mantra...
"I will focus on my breath, allowing it
to be a source of calm and balance.
I inhale positive energy and exhale any
tension or negativity as I drift off to sleep."

Good Morning

Set your intentions to reinforce a health and positive mindset the
moment you wake up and repeat this morning meditation mantra:
"I start this day with love for myself, I am mindful of my wellbeing,
and I will make choices for a healthy and balanced life."

DAILY CHECK-IN

Mind
I will nurture and build my emotional health and resilience by...

....

Body
I will nourish, celebrate, and empower my body by...

....

Soul
I will create moments of tranquility, peace, and harmony by...

....

I will find harmony and
balance in nature by...

....

....

....

....

....

I set a positive intention to...

....

....

....

....

....

Sweet Dreams

Before you go to sleep at night, light a scented candle,
put on some calming music, and take some time out for reflection...

What I loved and appreciated about myself today was...

....

....

The negative thoughts that I release are...

....

....

REFLECTIONS

Three moments that brought joy, laughter or a sense of fulfilment were...

1 ....

2 ....

3 ....

My good night meditation mantra...
"I will focus on my breath, allowing it
to be a source of calm and balance.
I inhale positive energy and exhale any
tension or negativity as I drift off to sleep."

Good Morning

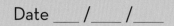

Date ___ / ___ / ___

Set your intentions to reinforce a health and positive mindset the
moment you wake up and repeat this morning meditation mantra:
"I start this day with love for myself, I am mindful of my wellbeing,
and I will make choices for a healthy and balanced life."

DAILY CHECK-IN

Mind
I will nurture and build my emotional health and resilience by...

....

Body
I will nourish, celebrate, and empower my body by...

....

Soul
I will create moments of tranquility, peace, and harmony by...

....

I will find harmony and
balance in nature by...

....

....

....

....

....

I set a positive intention to...

....

....

....

....

....

Sweet Dreams

Before you go to sleep at night, light a scented candle,
put on some calming music, and take some time out for reflection...

What I loved and appreciated about myself today was...

....

....

The negative thoughts that I release are...

....

....

REFLECTIONS

Three moments that brought joy, laughter or a sense of fulfilment were...

1 ....

2 ....

3 ....

My good night meditation mantra...
"I will focus on my breath, allowing it
to be a source of calm and balance.
I inhale positive energy and exhale any
tension or negativity as I drift off to sleep."

Good Morning

Set your intentions to reinforce a health and positive mindset the
moment you wake up and repeat this morning meditation mantra:
"I start this day with love for myself, I am mindful of my wellbeing,
and I will make choices for a healthy and balanced life."

DAILY CHECK-IN

Mind
I will nurture and build my emotional health and resilience by...

....

Body
I will nourish, celebrate, and empower my body by...

....

Soul
I will create moments of tranquility, peace, and harmony by...

....

I will find harmony and
balance in nature by...

....

....

....

....

....

I set a positive intention to...

....

....

....

....

....

Sweet Dreams

Before you go to sleep at night, light a scented candle,
put on some calming music, and take some time out for reflection...

What I loved and appreciated about myself today was...

....

....

The negative thoughts that I release are...

....

....

REFLECTIONS

Three moments that brought joy, laughter or a sense of fulfilment were...

1 ....

2 ....

3 ....

My good night meditation mantra...
"I will focus on my breath, allowing it
to be a source of calm and balance.
I inhale positive energy and exhale any
tension or negativity as I drift off to sleep."

Good Morning

Set your intentions to reinforce a health and positive mindset the moment you wake up and repeat this morning meditation mantra: "I start this day with love for myself, I am mindful of my wellbeing, and I will make choices for a healthy and balanced life."

DAILY CHECK-IN

Mind
I will nurture and build my emotional health and resilience by...

....

Body
I will nourish, celebrate, and empower my body by...

....

Soul
I will create moments of tranquility, peace, and harmony by...

....

I will find harmony and
balance in nature by...

....

....

....

....

....

....

I set a positive intention to...

....

....

....

....

....

....

Sweet Dreams

Before you go to sleep at night, light a scented candle,
put on some calming music, and take some time out for reflection...

What I loved and appreciated about myself today was...

....

....

The negative thoughts that I release are...

....

....

REFLECTIONS

Three moments that brought joy, laughter or a sense of fulfilment were...

1 ....

2 ....

3 ....

My good night meditation mantra...
"I will focus on my breath, allowing it
to be a source of calm and balance.
I inhale positive energy and exhale any
tension or negativity as I drift off to sleep."

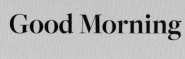

Good Morning

Date ___ /___ /___

Set your intentions to reinforce a health and positive mindset the moment you wake up and repeat this morning meditation mantra: "I start this day with love for myself, I am mindful of my wellbeing, and I will make choices for a healthy and balanced life."

DAILY CHECK-IN

Mind
I will nurture and build my emotional health and resilience by...

....

Body
I will nourish, celebrate, and empower my body by...

....

Soul
I will create moments of tranquility, peace, and harmony by...

....

I will find harmony and balance in nature by...

....

....

....

....

....

I set a positive intention to...

....

....

....

....

....

Sweet Dreams

Before you go to sleep at night, light a scented candle,
put on some calming music, and take some time out for reflection...

What I loved and appreciated about myself today was...

....

....

The negative thoughts that I release are...

....

....

REFLECTIONS

Three moments that brought joy, laughter or a sense of fulfilment were...

1 ....

2 ....

3 ....

My good night meditation mantra...
"I will focus on my breath, allowing it
to be a source of calm and balance.
I inhale positive energy and exhale any
tension or negativity as I drift off to sleep."

Good Morning

Set your intentions to reinforce a health and positive mindset the moment you wake up and repeat this morning meditation mantra: "I start this day with love for myself, I am mindful of my wellbeing, and I will make choices for a healthy and balanced life."

DAILY CHECK-IN

Mind
I will nurture and build my emotional health and resilience by...

....

Body
I will nourish, celebrate, and empower my body by...

....

Soul
I will create moments of tranquility, peace, and harmony by...

....

I will find harmony and balance in nature by...

....

....

....

....

....

I set a positive intention to...

....

....

....

....

....

Sweet Dreams

Before you go to sleep at night, light a scented candle,
put on some calming music, and take some time out for reflection...

What I loved and appreciated about myself today was...

....

....

The negative thoughts that I release are...

....

....

REFLECTIONS

Three moments that brought joy, laughter or a sense of fulfilment were...

1 ....

2 ....

3 ....

My good night meditation mantra...
"I will focus on my breath, allowing it
to be a source of calm and balance.
I inhale positive energy and exhale any
tension or negativity as I drift off to sleep."

Good Morning

Date ___ / ___ / ___

Set your intentions to reinforce a health and positive mindset the moment you wake up and repeat this morning meditation mantra: "I start this day with love for myself, I am mindful of my wellbeing, and I will make choices for a healthy and balanced life."

DAILY CHECK-IN

Mind
I will nurture and build my emotional health and resilience by...

....

Body
I will nourish, celebrate, and empower my body by...

....

Soul
I will create moments of tranquility, peace, and harmony by...

....

I will find harmony and balance in nature by...

....

....

....

....

....

I set a positive intention to...

....

....

....

....

....

....

Sweet Dreams

Before you go to sleep at night, light a scented candle,
put on some calming music, and take some time out for reflection...

What I loved and appreciated about myself today was...

....

....

The negative thoughts that I release are...

....

....

REFLECTIONS

Three moments that brought joy, laughter or a sense of fulfilment were...

1 ....

2 ....

3 ....

My good night meditation mantra...
"I will focus on my breath, allowing it
to be a source of calm and balance.
I inhale positive energy and exhale any
tension or negativity as I drift off to sleep."

Good Morning

Date ___ /___ /___

Set your intentions to reinforce a health and positive mindset the moment you wake up and repeat this morning meditation mantra: "I start this day with love for myself, I am mindful of my wellbeing, and I will make choices for a healthy and balanced life."

DAILY CHECK-IN

Mind
I will nurture and build my emotional health and resilience by...

....

Body
I will nourish, celebrate, and empower my body by...

....

Soul
I will create moments of tranquility, peace, and harmony by...

....

I will find harmony and balance in nature by...

....
....
....
....
....

I set a positive intention to...

....
....
....
....
....

Sweet Dreams

Before you go to sleep at night, light a scented candle,
put on some calming music, and take some time out for reflection...

What I loved and appreciated
about myself today was...

....

....

The negative thoughts that I release are...

....

....

REFLECTIONS

Three moments that brought joy, laughter or a sense of fulfilment were...

1 ....

2 ....

3 ....

My good night meditation mantra...
"I will focus on my breath, allowing it
to be a source of calm and balance.
I inhale positive energy and exhale any
tension or negativity as I drift off to sleep."

Good Morning

Date ___ / ___ / ___

Set your intentions to reinforce a health and positive mindset the moment you wake up and repeat this morning meditation mantra: "I start this day with love for myself, I am mindful of my wellbeing, and I will make choices for a healthy and balanced life."

DAILY CHECK-IN

Mind

I will nurture and build my emotional health and resilience by...

....

....

....

Body

I will nourish, celebrate, and empower my body by...

....

....

....

Soul

I will create moments of tranquility, peace, and harmony by...

....

....

....

I will find harmony and balance in nature by...

....

....

....

I set a positive intention to...

....

....

....

Sweet Dreams

What I loved and appreciated about myself today was...

....

....

....

....

Before you go to sleep at night, light a scented candle, put on some calming music, and take some time out for reflection...

The negative thoughts that I release are...

....

....

REFLECTIONS

Three moments that brought joy, laughter or a sense of fulfilment were...

1 ....

2 ....

3 ....

My good night meditation mantra...
"I will focus on my breath, allowing it to be a source of calm and balance. I inhale positive energy and exhale any tension or negativity as I drift off to sleep."

Good Morning

Set your intentions to reinforce a health and positive mindset the
moment you wake up and repeat this morning meditation mantra:
"I start this day with love for myself, I am mindful of my wellbeing,
and I will make choices for a healthy and balanced life."

DAILY CHECK-IN

Mind

I will nurture and
build my emotional health
and resilience by...

....

....

....

Body

I will nourish,
celebrate, and empower
my body by...

....

....

....

Soul

I will create
moments of tranquility,
peace, and harmony by...

....

....

....

I will find
harmony and
balance in nature by...

....

....

....

I set a positive
intention to...

....

....

....

Sweet Dreams

What I loved and appreciated
about myself today was...

Before you go to
sleep at night, light a
scented candle, put on
some calming music, and
take some time out for
reflection...

....

....

....

....

The negative thoughts that I release are...

....

....

REFLECTIONS

Three moments that brought joy,
laughter or a sense of fulfilment were...

1 ....

2 ....

3 ....

My good night
meditation mantra...
"I will focus on my breath,
allowing it to be a source of calm
and balance. I inhale positive
energy and exhale any tension
or negativity as I drift
off to sleep."

Good Morning

Set your intentions to reinforce a health and positive mindset the moment you wake up and repeat this morning meditation mantra: "I start this day with love for myself, I am mindful of my wellbeing, and I will make choices for a healthy and balanced life."

DAILY CHECK-IN

Mind

I will nurture and build my emotional health and resilience by...

....

....

....

Body

I will nourish, celebrate, and empower my body by...

....

....

....

Soul

I will create moments of tranquility, peace, and harmony by...

....

....

....

I will find harmony and balance in nature by...

....

....

....

I set a positive intention to...

....

....

....

Sweet Dreams

Before you go to sleep at night, light a scented candle, put on some calming music, and take some time out for reflection...

What I loved and appreciated about myself today was...

....

....

....

....

The negative thoughts that I release are...

....

....

REFLECTIONS

Three moments that brought joy, laughter or a sense of fulfilment were...

1 ....

2 ....

3 ....

My good night meditation mantra...
"I will focus on my breath, allowing it to be a source of calm and balance. I inhale positive energy and exhale any tension or negativity as I drift off to sleep."

Good Morning

Set your intentions to reinforce a health and positive mindset the
moment you wake up and repeat this morning meditation mantra:
"I start this day with love for myself, I am mindful of my wellbeing,
and I will make choices for a healthy and balanced life."

DAILY CHECK-IN

Mind

I will nurture and
build my emotional health
and resilience by...

....

....

....

Body

I will nourish,
celebrate, and empower
my body by...

....

....

....

Soul

I will create
moments of tranquility,
peace, and harmony by...

....

....

....

I will find
harmony and
balance in nature by...

....

....

....

I set a positive
intention to...

....

....

....

Sweet Dreams

What I loved and appreciated
about myself today was...

Before you go to
sleep at night, light a
scented candle, put on
some calming music, and
take some time out for
reflection...

....

....

....

The negative thoughts that I release are...

....

....

REFLECTIONS

Three moments that brought joy,
laughter or a sense of fulfilment were...

1 ....

2 ....

3 ....

My good night
meditation mantra...
"I will focus on my breath,
allowing it to be a source of calm
and balance. I inhale positive
energy and exhale any tension
or negativity as I drift
off to sleep."

Good Morning

Date ___ / ___ / ___

Set your intentions to reinforce a health and positive mindset the moment you wake up and repeat this morning meditation mantra: "I start this day with love for myself, I am mindful of my wellbeing, and I will make choices for a healthy and balanced life."

DAILY CHECK-IN

Mind

I will nurture and build my emotional health and resilience by...

....

....

....

Body

I will nourish, celebrate, and empower my body by...

....

....

....

Soul

I will create moments of tranquility, peace, and harmony by...

....

....

....

I will find harmony and balance in nature by...

....

....

....

I set a positive intention to...

....

....

....

Sweet Dreams

What I loved and appreciated
about myself today was...

....

....

....

....

Before you go to
sleep at night, light a
scented candle, put on
some calming music, and
take some time out for
reflection...

The negative thoughts that I release are...

....

....

REFLECTIONS

Three moments that brought joy,
laughter or a sense of fulfilment were...

1 ....

2 ....

3 ....

My good night
meditation mantra...
"I will focus on my breath,
allowing it to be a source of calm
and balance. I inhale positive
energy and exhale any tension
or negativity as I drift
off to sleep."

Good Morning

Set your intentions to reinforce a health and positive mindset the
moment you wake up and repeat this morning meditation mantra:
"I start this day with love for myself, I am mindful of my wellbeing,
and I will make choices for a healthy and balanced life."

DAILY CHECK-IN

Mind

I will nurture and
build my emotional health
and resilience by...

....

....

....

Body

I will nourish,
celebrate, and empower
my body by...

....

....

Soul

I will create
moments of tranquility,
peace, and harmony by...

....

....

....

I will find
harmony and
balance in nature by...

....

....

....

I set a positive
intention to...

....

....

....

Sweet Dreams

Before you go to sleep at night, light a scented candle, put on some calming music, and take some time out for reflection...

What I loved and appreciated about myself today was...

....

....

....

....

The negative thoughts that I release are...

....

....

REFLECTIONS

Three moments that brought joy, laughter or a sense of fulfilment were...

1 ....

2 ....

3 ....

My good night meditation mantra...
"I will focus on my breath, allowing it to be a source of calm and balance. I inhale positive energy and exhale any tension or negativity as I drift off to sleep."

Good Morning

Set your intentions to reinforce a health and positive mindset the
moment you wake up and repeat this morning meditation mantra:
"I start this day with love for myself, I am mindful of my wellbeing,
and I will make choices for a healthy and balanced life."

DAILY CHECK-IN

Mind

I will nurture and
build my emotional health
and resilience by...

....

....

....

Body

I will nourish,
celebrate, and empower
my body by...

....

....

....

Soul

I will create
moments of tranquility,
peace, and harmony by...

....

....

....

I will find
harmony and
balance in nature by...

....

....

....

I set a positive
intention to...

....

....

....

Sweet Dreams

What I loved and appreciated
about myself today was...

Before you go to
sleep at night, light a
scented candle, put on
some calming music, and
take some time out for
reflection...

....

....

....

....

The negative thoughts that I release are...

....

....

REFLECTIONS

Three moments that brought joy,
laughter or a sense of fulfilment were...

1 ....

2 ....

3 ....

**My good night
meditation mantra...**
"I will focus on my breath,
allowing it to be a source of calm
and balance. I inhale positive
energy and exhale any tension
or negativity as I drift
off to sleep."

Good Morning

Set your intentions to reinforce a health and positive mindset the
moment you wake up and repeat this morning meditation mantra:
"I start this day with love for myself, I am mindful of my wellbeing,
and I will make choices for a healthy and balanced life."

DAILY CHECK-IN

Mind
I will nurture and
build my emotional health
and resilience by...

....

....

....

Body
I will nourish,
celebrate, and empower
my body by...

....

....

....

Soul
I will create
moments of tranquility,
peace, and harmony by...

....

....

....

I will find
harmony and
balance in nature by...

....

....

....

I set a positive
intention to...

....

....

....

Sweet Dreams

Before you go to sleep at night, light a scented candle, put on some calming music, and take some time out for reflection...

What I loved and appreciated about myself today was...

....

....

....

....

The negative thoughts that I release are...

....

....

REFLECTIONS

Three moments that brought joy, laughter or a sense of fulfilment were...

1 ....

2 ....

3 ....

My good night meditation mantra...
"I will focus on my breath, allowing it to be a source of calm and balance. I inhale positive energy and exhale any tension or negativity as I drift off to sleep."

Good Morning

Date ___ / ___ / ___

Set your intentions to reinforce a health and positive mindset the moment you wake up and repeat this morning meditation mantra: "I start this day with love for myself, I am mindful of my wellbeing, and I will make choices for a healthy and balanced life."

DAILY CHECK-IN

Mind
I will nurture and build my emotional health and resilience by...

....
....
....

Body
I will nourish, celebrate, and empower my body by...

....
....
....

Soul
I will create moments of tranquility, peace, and harmony by...

....
....

I will find harmony and balance in nature by...

....
....
....

I set a positive intention to...

....
....
....

Sweet Dreams

Before you go to sleep at night, light a scented candle, put on some calming music, and take some time out for reflection...

What I loved and appreciated about myself today was...

....

....

....

....

The negative thoughts that I release are...

....

....

REFLECTIONS

Three moments that brought joy, laughter or a sense of fulfilment were...

1 ....

2 ....

3 ....

My good night meditation mantra...
"I will focus on my breath, allowing it to be a source of calm and balance. I inhale positive energy and exhale any tension or negativity as I drift off to sleep."

Good Morning

Date ___ / ___ / ___

Set your intentions to reinforce a health and positive mindset the moment you wake up and repeat this morning meditation mantra: "I start this day with love for myself, I am mindful of my wellbeing, and I will make choices for a healthy and balanced life."

DAILY CHECK-IN

Mind
I will nurture and build my emotional health and resilience by...

....

....

Body
I will nourish, celebrate, and empower my body by...

....

....

Soul
I will create moments of tranquility, peace, and harmony by...

....

....

....

I will find harmony and balance in nature by...

....

....

....

I set a positive intention to...

....

....

....

Sweet Dreams

What I loved and appreciated
about myself today was...

Before you go to
sleep at night, light a
scented candle, put on
some calming music, and
take some time out for
reflection...

....

....

....

....

The negative thoughts that I release are...

....

....

REFLECTIONS
Three moments that brought joy,
laughter or a sense of fulfilment were...

My good night
meditation mantra...
"I will focus on my breath,
allowing it to be a source of calm
and balance. I inhale positive
energy and exhale any tension
or negativity as I drift
off to sleep."

1 ....

2 ....

3 ....

Good Morning

Date ___ / ___ / ___

Set your intentions to reinforce a health and positive mindset the moment you wake up and repeat this morning meditation mantra: "I start this day with love for myself, I am mindful of my wellbeing, and I will make choices for a healthy and balanced life."

DAILY CHECK-IN

Mind

I will nurture and build my emotional health and resilience by...

....

....

....

Body

I will nourish, celebrate, and empower my body by...

....

....

....

Soul

I will create moments of tranquility, peace, and harmony by...

....

....

....

I will find harmony and balance in nature by...

....

....

....

I set a positive intention to...

....

....

....

Sweet Dreams

Before you go to sleep at night, light a scented candle, put on some calming music, and take some time out for reflection...

What I loved and appreciated about myself today was...

....

....

....

....

The negative thoughts that I release are...

....

....

REFLECTIONS

Three moments that brought joy, laughter or a sense of fulfilment were...

1 ....

2 ....

3 ....

My good night meditation mantra...
"I will focus on my breath, allowing it to be a source of calm and balance. I inhale positive energy and exhale any tension or negativity as I drift off to sleep."

Good Morning

Date ___ / ___ / ___

Set your intentions to reinforce a health and positive mindset the moment you wake up and repeat this morning meditation mantra: "I start this day with love for myself, I am mindful of my wellbeing, and I will make choices for a healthy and balanced life."

DAILY CHECK-IN

Mind

I will nurture and build my emotional health and resilience by...

....

....

....

Body

I will nourish, celebrate, and empower my body by...

....

....

....

Soul

I will create moments of tranquility, peace, and harmony by...

....

....

....

I will find harmony and balance in nature by...

....

....

....

I set a positive intention to...

....

....

....

Sweet Dreams

What I loved and appreciated
about myself today was...

Before you go to
sleep at night, light a
scented candle, put on
some calming music, and
take some time out for
reflection...

....

....

....

....

The negative thoughts that I release are...

....

....

REFLECTIONS

Three moments that brought joy,
laughter or a sense of fulfilment were...

My good night
meditation mantra...
"I will focus on my breath,
allowing it to be a source of calm
and balance. I inhale positive
energy and exhale any tension
or negativity as I drift
off to sleep."

1 ....

2 ....

3 ....

Good Morning

Set your intentions to reinforce a health and positive mindset the
moment you wake up and repeat this morning meditation mantra:
"I start this day with love for myself, I am mindful of my wellbeing,
and I will make choices for a healthy and balanced life."

DAILY CHECK-IN

Mind

I will nurture and
build my emotional health
and resilience by...

....

....

....

Body

I will nourish,
celebrate, and empower
my body by...

....

....

....

Soul

I will create
moments of tranquility,
peace, and harmony by...

....

....

....

I will find
harmony and
balance in nature by...

....

....

....

I set a positive
intention to...

....

....

....

Sweet Dreams

What I loved and appreciated about myself today was...

Before you go to sleep at night, light a scented candle, put on some calming music, and take some time out for reflection...

....

....

....

....

The negative thoughts that I release are...

....

....

REFLECTIONS

Three moments that brought joy, laughter or a sense of fulfilment were...

1 ....

2 ....

3 ....

My good night meditation mantra...
"I will focus on my breath, allowing it to be a source of calm and balance. I inhale positive energy and exhale any tension or negativity as I drift off to sleep."

Good Morning

Date ___ / ___ / ___

Set your intentions
to reinforce a health and
positive mindset the moment
you wake up and repeat this
morning meditation mantra:

"I start this day with love for
myself, I am mindful of my
wellbeing, and I will make
choices for a healthy and
balanced life."

I will find harmony and

balance in nature by...

....
....
....
....

I set a positive

intention to...

....
....
....
....

DAILY CHECK-IN

Mind
I will nurture and build my
emotional health and resilience by...

....
....
....

Body
I will nourish, celebrate,
and empower my body by...

....
....
....

Soul
I will create moments of tranquility,
peace, and harmony by...

....
....
....

Sweet Dreams

Before you go to sleep at night, light a scented candle,
put on some calming music, and take some time out for reflection...

What I loved
and appreciated about
myself today was...

....

....

....

....

The negative thoughts
that I release are...

....

....

....

....

....

REFLECTIONS

Three moments that brought joy, laughter or a sense of fulfilment were...

1 ....

2 ....

3 ....

My good night meditation mantra...
"I will focus on my breath, allowing it to be a source of calm and balance.
I inhale positive energy and exhale any tension or negativity as I drift off to sleep."

Good Morning

Date ___ / ___ / ___

Set your intentions to reinforce a health and positive mindset the moment you wake up and repeat this morning meditation mantra:

"I start this day with love for myself, I am mindful of my wellbeing, and I will make choices for a healthy and balanced life."

I will find harmony and balance in nature by...

....

....

....

I set a positive intention to...

....

....

....

....

DAILY CHECK-IN

Mind
I will nurture and build my emotional health and resilience by...

....

....

....

Body
I will nourish, celebrate, and empower my body by...

....

....

....

Soul
I will create moments of tranquility, peace, and harmony by...

....

....

....

Sweet Dreams

Before you go to sleep at night, light a scented candle,
put on some calming music, and take some time out for reflection...

What I loved
and appreciated about
myself today was...

....

....

....

....

The negative thoughts
that I release are...

....

....

....

....

....

REFLECTIONS

Three moments that brought joy, laughter or a sense of fulfilment were...

1 ....

2 ....

3 ....

My good night meditation mantra...
"I will focus on my breath, allowing it to be a source of calm and balance.
I inhale positive energy and exhale any tension or negativity as I drift off to sleep."

Good Morning

Date ___ /___ /___

Set your intentions to reinforce a health and positive mindset the moment you wake up and repeat this morning meditation mantra:

"I start this day with love for myself, I am mindful of my wellbeing, and I will make choices for a healthy and balanced life."

I will find harmony and balance in nature by...

....

....

....

....

I set a positive intention to...

....

....

....

....

DAILY CHECK-IN

Mind
I will nurture and build my emotional health and resilience by...

....

....

....

Body
I will nourish, celebrate, and empower my body by...

....

....

....

Soul
I will create moments of tranquility, peace, and harmony by...

....

....

....

Sweet Dreams

Before you go to sleep at night, light a scented candle,
put on some calming music, and take some time out for reflection...

What I loved
and appreciated about
myself today was...

....

....

....

....

The negative thoughts
that I release are...

....

....

....

....

....

REFLECTIONS

Three moments that brought joy, laughter or a sense of fulfilment were...

1 ....

2 ....

3 ....

My good night meditation mantra...
"I will focus on my breath, allowing it to be a source of calm and balance.
I inhale positive energy and exhale any tension or negativity as I drift off to sleep."

Good Morning

Date ___ / ___ / ___

Set your intentions to reinforce a health and positive mindset the moment you wake up and repeat this morning meditation mantra:

"I start this day with love for myself, I am mindful of my wellbeing, and I will make choices for a healthy and balanced life."

I will find harmony and balance in nature by...

....

....

....

I set a positive intention to...

....

....

....

....

DAILY CHECK-IN

Mind
I will nurture and build my emotional health and resilience by...

....

....

....

Body
I will nourish, celebrate, and empower my body by...

....

....

....

Soul
I will create moments of tranquility, peace, and harmony by...

....

....

....

Sweet Dreams

Before you go to sleep at night, light a scented candle,
put on some calming music, and take some time out for reflection...

What I loved
and appreciated about
myself today was...

....

....

....

....

The negative thoughts
that I release are...

....

....

....

....

....

REFLECTIONS

Three moments that brought joy, laughter or a sense of fulfilment were...

1 ....

2 ....

3 ....

My good night meditation mantra...
"I will focus on my breath, allowing it to be a source of calm and balance.
I inhale positive energy and exhale any tension or negativity as I drift off to sleep."

Good Morning

Date ___ /___ /___

Set your intentions
to reinforce a health and
positive mindset the moment
you wake up and repeat this
morning meditation mantra:

"I start this day with love for
myself, I am mindful of my
wellbeing, and I will make
choices for a healthy and
balanced life."

I will find harmony and

balance in nature by...

....

....

....

....

I set a positive

intention to...

....

....

....

....

DAILY CHECK-IN

Mind
I will nurture and build my
emotional health and resilience by...

....

....

....

Body
I will nourish, celebrate,
and empower my body by...

....

....

....

Soul
I will create moments of tranquility,
peace, and harmony by...

....

....

....

Sweet Dreams

Before you go to sleep at night, light a scented candle,
put on some calming music, and take some time out for reflection...

What I loved
and appreciated about
myself today was...

....

....

....

....

The negative thoughts
that I release are...

....

....

....

....

....

REFLECTIONS

Three moments that brought joy, laughter or a sense of fulfilment were...

1 ....

2 ....

3 ....

My good night meditation mantra...
"I will focus on my breath, allowing it to be a source of calm and balance.
I inhale positive energy and exhale any tension or negativity as I drift off to sleep."

Good Morning

Date ___ /___ /___

Set your intentions to reinforce a health and positive mindset the moment you wake up and repeat this morning meditation mantra:

"I start this day with love for myself, I am mindful of my wellbeing, and I will make choices for a healthy and balanced life."

I will find harmony and balance in nature by...

....

....

....

....

I set a positive intention to...

....

....

....

....

DAILY CHECK-IN

Mind
I will nurture and build my emotional health and resilience by...

....

....

....

Body
I will nourish, celebrate, and empower my body by...

....

....

....

Soul
I will create moments of tranquility, peace, and harmony by...

....

....

....

Sweet Dreams

Before you go to sleep at night, light a scented candle,
put on some calming music, and take some time out for reflection...

What I loved
and appreciated about
myself today was...

....

....

....

....

The negative thoughts
that I release are...

....

....

....

....

....

REFLECTIONS

Three moments that brought joy, laughter or a sense of fulfilment were...

1 ....

2 ....

3 ....

My good night meditation mantra...
"I will focus on my breath, allowing it to be a source of calm and balance.
I inhale positive energy and exhale any tension or negativity as I drift off to sleep."

Good Morning

Date ___ / ___ / ___

Set your intentions to reinforce a health and positive mindset the moment you wake up and repeat this morning meditation mantra:

"I start this day with love for myself, I am mindful of my wellbeing, and I will make choices for a healthy and balanced life."

I will find harmony and balance in nature by...

....

....

....

I set a positive intention to...

....

....

....

....

DAILY CHECK-IN

Mind
I will nurture and build my emotional health and resilience by...

....

....

....

Body
I will nourish, celebrate, and empower my body by...

....

....

....

Soul
I will create moments of tranquility, peace, and harmony by...

....

....

....

Sweet Dreams

Before you go to sleep at night, light a scented candle,
put on some calming music, and take some time out for reflection...

What I loved
and appreciated about
myself today was...

....

....

....

....

The negative thoughts
that I release are...

....

....

....

....

....

REFLECTIONS

Three moments that brought joy, laughter or a sense of fulfilment were...

1 ....

2 ....

3 ....

My good night meditation mantra...
"I will focus on my breath, allowing it to be a source of calm and balance.
I inhale positive energy and exhale any tension or negativity as I drift off to sleep."

Good Morning

Date ___ / ___ / ___

Set your intentions to reinforce a health and positive mindset the moment you wake up and repeat this morning meditation mantra:

"I start this day with love for myself, I am mindful of my wellbeing, and I will make choices for a healthy and balanced life."

I will find harmony and balance in nature by...

....

....

....

....

I set a positive intention to...

....

....

....

....

DAILY CHECK-IN

Mind
I will nurture and build my emotional health and resilience by...

....

....

....

Body
I will nourish, celebrate, and empower my body by...

....

....

....

Soul
I will create moments of tranquility, peace, and harmony by...

....

....

....

Sweet Dreams

What I loved
and appreciated about
myself today was...

....

....

....

....

The negative thoughts
that I release are...

....

....

....

....

....

REFLECTIONS

Three moments that brought joy, laughter or a sense of fulfilment were...

1 ....

2 ....

3 ....

My good night meditation mantra...
"I will focus on my breath, allowing it to be a source of calm and balance.
I inhale positive energy and exhale any tension or negativity as I drift off to sleep."

Good Morning

Date ___ / ___ / ___

Set your intentions to reinforce a health and positive mindset the moment you wake up and repeat this morning meditation mantra:

"I start this day with love for myself, I am mindful of my wellbeing, and I will make choices for a healthy and balanced life."

I will find harmony and balance in nature by...

....
....
....

I set a positive intention to...

....
....
....
....

DAILY CHECK-IN

Mind
I will nurture and build my emotional health and resilience by...

....
....
....

Body
I will nourish, celebrate, and empower my body by...

....
....
....

Soul
I will create moments of tranquility, peace, and harmony by...

....
....
....

Sweet Dreams

Before you go to sleep at night, light a scented candle,
put on some calming music, and take some time out for reflection...

What I loved
and appreciated about
myself today was...

....

....

....

....

The negative thoughts
that I release are...

....

....

....

....

....

REFLECTIONS

Three moments that brought joy, laughter or a sense of fulfilment were...

1 ....

2 ....

3 ....

My good night meditation mantra...
"I will focus on my breath, allowing it to be a source of calm and balance.
I inhale positive energy and exhale any tension or negativity as I drift off to sleep."

Good Morning

Date ___ / ___ / ___

Set your intentions to reinforce a health and positive mindset the moment you wake up and repeat this morning meditation mantra:

"I start this day with love for myself, I am mindful of my wellbeing, and I will make choices for a healthy and balanced life."

I will find harmony and balance in nature by...

....
....
....

I set a positive intention to...

....
....
....
....

DAILY CHECK-IN

Mind
I will nurture and build my emotional health and resilience by...

....
....
....

Body
I will nourish, celebrate, and empower my body by...

....
....
....

Soul
I will create moments of tranquility, peace, and harmony by...

....
....
....

Sweet Dreams

Before you go to sleep at night, light a scented candle,
put on some calming music, and take some time out for reflection...

What I loved
and appreciated about
myself today was...

....

....

....

....

The negative thoughts
that I release are...

....

....

....

....

....

REFLECTIONS

Three moments that brought joy, laughter or a sense of fulfilment were...

1 ....

2 ....

3 ....

My good night meditation mantra...
"I will focus on my breath, allowing it to be a source of calm and balance.
I inhale positive energy and exhale any tension or negativity as I drift off to sleep."

Good Morning

Date ___ / ___ / ___

Set your intentions to reinforce a health and positive mindset the moment you wake up and repeat this morning meditation mantra:

"I start this day with love for myself, I am mindful of my wellbeing, and I will make choices for a healthy and balanced life."

I will find harmony and balance in nature by...

....

....

....

....

I set a positive intention to...

....

....

....

....

DAILY CHECK-IN

Mind
I will nurture and build my emotional health and resilience by...

....

....

....

Body
I will nourish, celebrate, and empower my body by...

....

....

....

Soul
I will create moments of tranquility, peace, and harmony by...

....

....

....

Sweet Dreams

Before you go to sleep at night, light a scented candle,
put on some calming music, and take some time out for reflection...

What I loved
and appreciated about
myself today was...

....

....

....

....

The negative thoughts
that I release are...

....

....

....

....

....

REFLECTIONS

Three moments that brought joy, laughter or a sense of fulfilment were...

1 ....

2 ....

3 ....

My good night meditation mantra...
"I will focus on my breath, allowing it to be a source of calm and balance.
I inhale positive energy and exhale any tension or negativity as I drift off to sleep."

Good Morning

Date ___ / ___ / ___

Set your intentions to reinforce a health and positive mindset the moment you wake up and repeat this morning meditation mantra:

"I start this day with love for myself, I am mindful of my wellbeing, and I will make choices for a healthy and balanced life."

I will find harmony and balance in nature by...

....
....
....
....

I set a positive intention to...

....
....
....
....

DAILY CHECK-IN

Mind
I will nurture and build my emotional health and resilience by...

....
....
....

Body
I will nourish, celebrate, and empower my body by...

....
....
....

Soul
I will create moments of tranquility, peace, and harmony by...

....
....
....

Sweet Dreams

Before you go to sleep at night, light a scented candle,
put on some calming music, and take some time out for reflection...

What I loved
and appreciated about
myself today was...

....

....

....

....

The negative thoughts
that I release are...

....

....

....

....

....

REFLECTIONS

Three moments that brought joy, laughter or a sense of fulfilment were...

1 ....

2 ....

3 ....

My good night meditation mantra...
"I will focus on my breath, allowing it to be a source of calm and balance.
I inhale positive energy and exhale any tension or negativity as I drift off to sleep."

Good Morning

Date ___ / ___ / ___

Set your intentions to reinforce a health and positive mindset the moment you wake up and repeat this morning meditation mantra:

"I start this day with love for myself, I am mindful of my wellbeing, and I will make choices for a healthy and balanced life."

I will find harmony and balance in nature by...

....

....

....

....

I set a positive intention to...

....

....

....

....

DAILY CHECK-IN

Mind
I will nurture and build my emotional health and resilience by...

....

....

....

Body
I will nourish, celebrate, and empower my body by...

....

....

....

Soul
I will create moments of tranquility, peace, and harmony by...

....

....

....

Sweet Dreams

Before you go to sleep at night, light a scented candle,
put on some calming music, and take some time out for reflection...

What I loved
and appreciated about
myself today was...

....

....

....

....

The negative thoughts
that I release are...

....

....

....

....

....

REFLECTIONS

Three moments that brought joy, laughter or a sense of fulfilment were...

1 ....

2 ....

3 ....

My good night meditation mantra...
"I will focus on my breath, allowing it to be a source of calm and balance.
I inhale positive energy and exhale any tension or negativity as I drift off to sleep."

Good Morning

Set your intentions to reinforce a health and positive mindset the
moment you wake up and repeat this morning meditation mantra:
"I start this day with love for myself, I am mindful of my wellbeing,
and I will make choices for a healthy and balanced life."

DAILY CHECK-IN

Mind
I will nurture and build my emotional health and resilience by...

....

Body
I will nourish, celebrate, and empower my body by...

....

Soul
I will create moments of

tranquility, peace, and harmony by...

....

....

> I will find
> harmony and
> balance in nature by...
>
> ....
>
> ....
>
> ....

I set a positive intention to...

....

Sweet Dreams

Before you go to sleep at night, light a scented candle, put on some calming music, and take some time out for reflection...

What I loved and appreciated about myself today was...

....

....

....

The negative thoughts that I release are...

....

....

....

REFLECTIONS

Three moments that brought joy, laughter or a sense of fulfilment were...

1 ....

2 ....

3 ....

My good night meditation mantra...
"I will focus on my breath, allowing it to be a source of
calm and balance. I inhale positive energy and exhale
any tension or negativity as I drift off to sleep."

Good Morning

Date ___ / ___ / ___

Set your intentions to reinforce a health and positive mindset the moment you wake up and repeat this morning meditation mantra: "I start this day with love for myself, I am mindful of my wellbeing, and I will make choices for a healthy and balanced life."

DAILY CHECK-IN

Mind
I will nurture and build my emotional health and resilience by...

....

Body
I will nourish, celebrate, and empower my body by...

....

Soul
I will create moments of

tranquility, peace, and harmony by...

....

....

I will find

harmony and

balance in nature by...

....

....

....

I set a positive intention to...

....

Sweet Dreams

Before you go to
sleep at night, light a scented
candle, put on some calming music,
and take some time out for
reflection...

What I loved and appreciated
about myself today was...

....

....

....

The negative thoughts that I release are...

....

....

....

REFLECTIONS

Three moments that brought joy, laughter or a sense of fulfilment were...

1 ....

2 ....

3 ....

My good night meditation mantra...
"I will focus on my breath, allowing it to be a source of
calm and balance. I inhale positive energy and exhale
any tension or negativity as I drift off to sleep."

Good Morning

Date ___ / ___ / ___

Set your intentions to reinforce a health and positive mindset the moment you wake up and repeat this morning meditation mantra: "I start this day with love for myself, I am mindful of my wellbeing, and I will make choices for a healthy and balanced life."

DAILY CHECK-IN

Mind
I will nurture and build my emotional health and resilience by...

....

Body
I will nourish, celebrate, and empower my body by...

....

Soul
I will create moments of

tranquility, peace, and harmony by...

....

....

I will find

harmony and

balance in nature by...

....

....

....

I set a positive intention to...

....

Sweet Dreams

Before you go to
sleep at night, light a scented
candle, put on some calming music,
and take some time out for
reflection...

What I loved and appreciated
about myself today was...

....
....
....

The negative thoughts that I release are...

....
....
....

REFLECTIONS

Three moments that brought joy, laughter or a sense of fulfilment were...

1 ....

2 ....

3 ....

My good night meditation mantra...
"I will focus on my breath, allowing it to be a source of
calm and balance. I inhale positive energy and exhale
any tension or negativity as I drift off to sleep."

Good Morning

Date ___ / ___ / ___

Set your intentions to reinforce a health and positive mindset the moment you wake up and repeat this morning meditation mantra: "I start this day with love for myself, I am mindful of my wellbeing, and I will make choices for a healthy and balanced life."

DAILY CHECK-IN

Mind
I will nurture and build my emotional health and resilience by...

....

Body
I will nourish, celebrate, and empower my body by...

....

Soul
I will create moments of
tranquility, peace, and harmony by...

....

....

I will find

harmony and

balance in nature by...

....

....

....

I set a positive intention to...

....

Sweet Dreams

Before you go to
sleep at night, light a scented
candle, put on some calming music,
and take some time out for
reflection...

What I loved and appreciated
about myself today was...

....

....

....

The negative thoughts that I release are...

....

....

....

REFLECTIONS
Three moments that brought joy, laughter or a sense of fulfilment were...

1 ....

2 ....

3 ....

My good night meditation mantra...
"I will focus on my breath, allowing it to be a source of
calm and balance. I inhale positive energy and exhale
any tension or negativity as I drift off to sleep."

Good Morning

Date ___ / ___ / ___

Set your intentions to reinforce a health and positive mindset the moment you wake up and repeat this morning meditation mantra: "I start this day with love for myself, I am mindful of my wellbeing, and I will make choices for a healthy and balanced life."

DAILY CHECK-IN

Mind
I will nurture and build my emotional health and resilience by...

....

Body
I will nourish, celebrate, and empower my body by...

....

Soul
I will create moments of
tranquility, peace, and harmony by...

....

....

I will find harmony and balance in nature by...

....

....

....

I set a positive intention to...

....

Sweet Dreams

Before you go to
sleep at night, light a scented
candle, put on some calming music,
and take some time out for
reflection...

What I loved and appreciated
about myself today was...

....

....

....

The negative thoughts that I release are...

....

....

....

REFLECTIONS

Three moments that brought joy, laughter or a sense of fulfilment were...

1 ....

2 ....

3 ....

My good night meditation mantra...
"I will focus on my breath, allowing it to be a source of
calm and balance. I inhale positive energy and exhale
any tension or negativity as I drift off to sleep."

Good Morning

Date ___ / ___ / ___

Set your intentions to reinforce a health and positive mindset the moment you wake up and repeat this morning meditation mantra: "I start this day with love for myself, I am mindful of my wellbeing, and I will make choices for a healthy and balanced life."

DAILY CHECK-IN

Mind
I will nurture and build my emotional health and resilience by...

....

Body
I will nourish, celebrate, and empower my body by...

....

Soul
I will create moments of
tranquility, peace, and harmony by...

....

....

I will find
harmony and
balance in nature by...

....

....

....

I set a positive intention to...

....

Sweet Dreams

Before you go to sleep at night, light a scented candle, put on some calming music, and take some time out for reflection...

What I loved and appreciated about myself today was...

....

....

....

The negative thoughts that I release are...

....

....

....

REFLECTIONS

Three moments that brought joy, laughter or a sense of fulfilment were...

1 ....

2 ....

3 ....

My good night meditation mantra...
"I will focus on my breath, allowing it to be a source of calm and balance. I inhale positive energy and exhale any tension or negativity as I drift off to sleep."

Good Morning

Date ___ / ___ / ___

Set your intentions to reinforce a health and positive mindset the moment you wake up and repeat this morning meditation mantra: "I start this day with love for myself, I am mindful of my wellbeing, and I will make choices for a healthy and balanced life."

DAILY CHECK-IN

Mind
I will nurture and build my emotional health and resilience by...

....

Body
I will nourish, celebrate, and empower my body by...

....

Soul
I will create moments of
tranquility, peace, and harmony by...

....

....

I will find
harmony and
balance in nature by...

....

....

....

I set a positive intention to...

....

Sweet Dreams

Before you go to
sleep at night, light a scented
candle, put on some calming music,
and take some time out for
reflection...

What I loved and appreciated
about myself today was...

....

....

....

The negative thoughts that I release are...

....

....

....

REFLECTIONS

Three moments that brought joy, laughter or a sense of fulfilment were...

1 ....

2 ....

3 ....

My good night meditation mantra...
"I will focus on my breath, allowing it to be a source of
calm and balance. I inhale positive energy and exhale
any tension or negativity as I drift off to sleep."

Good Morning

Set your intentions to reinforce a health and positive mindset the moment you wake up and repeat this morning meditation mantra: "I start this day with love for myself, I am mindful of my wellbeing, and I will make choices for a healthy and balanced life."

DAILY CHECK-IN

Mind
I will nurture and build my emotional health and resilience by...

....

Body
I will nourish, celebrate, and empower my body by...

....

Soul
I will create moments of
tranquility, peace, and harmony by...

....

....

I will find
harmony and
balance in nature by...

....
....
....

I set a positive intention to...

....

Sweet Dreams

Before you go to sleep at night, light a scented candle, put on some calming music, and take some time out for reflection...

What I loved and appreciated about myself today was...

....

....

....

The negative thoughts that I release are...

....

....

....

REFLECTIONS

Three moments that brought joy, laughter or a sense of fulfilment were...

1 ....

2 ....

3 ....

My good night meditation mantra...
"I will focus on my breath, allowing it to be a source of
calm and balance. I inhale positive energy and exhale
any tension or negativity as I drift off to sleep."

Good Morning

Date ___ / ___ / ___

Set your intentions to reinforce a health and positive mindset the moment you wake up and repeat this morning meditation mantra: "I start this day with love for myself, I am mindful of my wellbeing, and I will make choices for a healthy and balanced life."

DAILY CHECK-IN

Mind

I will nurture and build my emotional health and resilience by...

....

Body

I will nourish, celebrate, and empower my body by...

....

Soul

I will create moments of
tranquility, peace, and harmony by...

....

....

I will find
harmony and
balance in nature by...

....

....

....

I set a positive intention to...

....

Sweet Dreams

Before you go to sleep at night, light a scented candle, put on some calming music, and take some time out for reflection...

What I loved and appreciated about myself today was...

....

....

....

The negative thoughts that I release are...

....

....

....

REFLECTIONS

Three moments that brought joy, laughter or a sense of fulfilment were...

1 ....

2 ....

3 ....

My good night meditation mantra...
"I will focus on my breath, allowing it to be a source of calm and balance. I inhale positive energy and exhale any tension or negativity as I drift off to sleep."

Good Morning

Date ___ / ___ / ___

Set your intentions to reinforce a health and positive mindset the moment you wake up and repeat this morning meditation mantra: "I start this day with love for myself, I am mindful of my wellbeing, and I will make choices for a healthy and balanced life."

DAILY CHECK-IN

Mind
I will nurture and build my emotional health and resilience by...

....

Body
I will nourish, celebrate, and empower my body by...

....

Soul
I will create moments of
tranquility, peace, and harmony by...

....

....

I will find
harmony and
balance in nature by...

....

....

....

I set a positive intention to...

....

Sweet Dreams

Before you go to sleep at night, light a scented candle, put on some calming music, and take some time out for reflection...

What I loved and appreciated about myself today was...

....

....

....

The negative thoughts that I release are...

....

....

....

REFLECTIONS

Three moments that brought joy, laughter or a sense of fulfilment were...

1 ....

2 ....

3 ....

My good night meditation mantra...
"I will focus on my breath, allowing it to be a source of calm and balance. I inhale positive energy and exhale any tension or negativity as I drift off to sleep."

Good Morning

Date ___ / ___ / ___

Set your intentions to reinforce a health and positive mindset the moment you wake up and repeat this morning meditation mantra: "I start this day with love for myself, I am mindful of my wellbeing, and I will make choices for a healthy and balanced life."

DAILY CHECK-IN

Mind
I will nurture and build my emotional health and resilience by...

....

Body
I will nourish, celebrate, and empower my body by...

....

Soul
I will create moments of

tranquility, peace, and harmony by...

....

....

I will find

harmony and

balance in nature by...

....

....

....

I set a positive intention to...

....

Sweet Dreams

Before you go to sleep at night, light a scented candle, put on some calming music, and take some time out for reflection...

What I loved and appreciated about myself today was...

....

....

....

The negative thoughts that I release are...

....

....

....

REFLECTIONS

Three moments that brought joy, laughter or a sense of fulfilment were...

1 ....

2 ....

3 ....

My good night meditation mantra...
"I will focus on my breath, allowing it to be a source of calm and balance. I inhale positive energy and exhale any tension or negativity as I drift off to sleep."